What Are Whales?

Milly Vranes

Momentum
What Are Whales?

First published in Great Britain in 1998 by

Folens Publishers
Albert House
Apex Business Centre
Boscombe Road
Dunstable
Beds LU5 4RL

© 1998 Momentum developed by Barrie Publishing Pty Limited
89 High St, Kew, Vic 3101, Australia
Reprinted 1999

Milly Vranes hereby asserts her moral right to be identified as the author of this work in accordance with the Copyright, Designs and Patents Act 1988.
© 1998 Folens Ltd. on behalf of the author.

All rights reserved. No part of this publication may be reproduced or transmitted in any form or by any means, electronic or mechanical, including photocopying, recording or any information storage and retrieval system, without written permission from the publisher.

British Library Cataloguing in Publication Data.
A Catalogue record for this book is available from the British Library

ISBN 1 86202 403 0

Designed by Pauline McClenahan
Printed in Singapore by PH Productions Pte Ltd

Every effort has been made to contact the owners of the photographs in this book. Where this has not been possible, we invite the owners of the copyright to notify the publishers.

A.N.T. Photo Library/Kelvin Aitken pp. 13, 17; A.N.T. Photo Library/Pete Atkinson p. 20; A.N.T. Photo Library/D. & V. Blagden p. 6; A.N.T. Photo Library/Ralph & Daffi Keller pp. 7, 22; A.N.T. Photo Library/Ron & Valerie Taylor p. 21; A.N.T. Photo Library/Barbara Todd cover, pp.20, 22; A.N.T. Photo Library/Nick Tonks p. 8; A.N.T. Photo Library/Dave Watts pp. 1, 7, 19, 21; Yanni Dellaportas p. 13; Horizon Photo Library pp. 4, 11; International Photographic Library pp. 5, 8, 9, 12, 14; Graham Meadows Photography pp. 10, 18.

Contents

Two Types of Whales	4
Whales Are Mammals	6
The Only Mammals to Live Entirely in Water	8
The Whale's Blowhole	10
The Pod	12
How Whales Communicate and Locate Food	14
The Whale's Ancestors	16
Why Are Whales So Interesting?	18
Whale Watching	20
Tips for Whale Watching	22
Glossary	23
Index	24

Two Types of Whales

Whales are creatures that have fascinated humans for centuries. There are two types of whales. These are toothed whales and baleen whales.

Toothed whales eat fish and squid. They use echolocation to find their food.

Sperm whales and pilot whales are types of toothed whales. So are dolphins and porpoises.

Baleen whales eat krill. These are small creatures that are like shrimp. The whales strain the krill through their baleen plates. This separates the krill from the seawater. Baleen whales need large amounts of krill to survive.

Humpback whales and right whales are types of baleen whales.

Whales Are Mammals

Whales are mammals. This means they are warm-blooded creatures. They feed their young milk.

Most large whales feed in Arctic and Antarctic waters. It is cold there, even in summer. They have a thick layer of fat called blubber. This helps them to keep warm. Whales move to warmer waters to mate and give birth to their calves.

The Only Mammals to Live Entirely in Water

Whales and their relatives, dolphins and porpoises, belong to the same mammal order. They are the only mammals to live their whole lives in water.

Humpback whales and right whales are large. But the blue whale is the largest mammal ever to have lived on Earth.

The ocean is the only place such large mammals can live. The water makes them buoyant. It supports their heavy weight.

The Whale's Blowhole

Whales breathe air as other mammals do. They do this through blowholes. Toothed whales have one blowhole. Baleen whales have two. The blowholes are on the top of their heads.

To breathe, the whale comes to the surface. It takes a deep breath of air. Its blowhole closes when it goes underwater. When the whale comes back to the surface, it lets out the air it has kept in its lungs. Then it takes another breath.

The whale does not blow water out through its blowhole, even though it might look as though it does. The air that has been in the whale's lungs has been warmed. When the whale breathes out, the warm air hits the cooler air outside. It turns into steam.

The Pod

Whales, like dolphins and porpoises, tend to stay in groups. A family group of whales is called a pod.

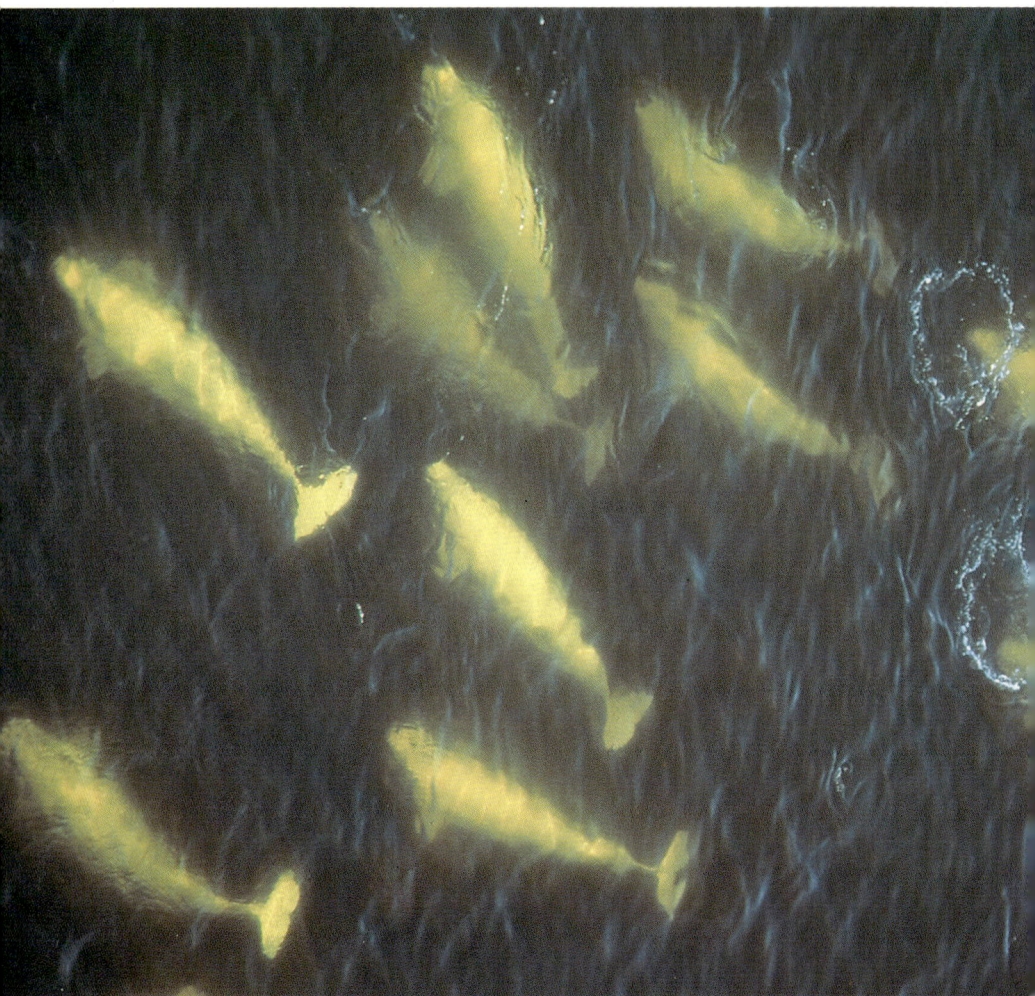

Each pod has a leader. The other members of the pod will follow their leader everywhere.

How Whales Communicate and Locate Food

Many scientists believe whales are very intelligent creatures. They communicate by making sounds. They can make a wide range of sounds.

Humpback whales string these sounds together. We call this a whale song. A whale song can last up to about 30 minutes.

Whales have poor eyesight. They have no sense of smell. They have keen senses of hearing and touch.

Toothed whales use sound to locate food. They use sound to sense their own location. They make a sound that is reflected off an object. This causes an echo. Whales can sense from the echo where the object is. This is called echolocation.

The Whale's Ancestors

Scientists believe that the ancestors of the whale once lived on land and had four legs. These creatures lived in the Cretaceous period. That was about 65 million years ago.

This is how scientists think the ancestor of the whale looked.

The skeleton of today's whale still shows signs that it once had back limbs.

Why Are Whales So Interesting?

Why do we find whales so interesting? It could be their huge size. It could be that they are able to communicate.

Scientists examining whales that have been washed ashore and died.

Scientists are studying whales and dolphins closely. They try to understand how they communicate. They are trying to understand why some whales get stranded on beaches.

Whale Watching

Have you ever seen a whale in its natural habitat? The humpback whale and the right whale are two types of large, slow-swimming whales that you might see.

Humpback whales have very long flippers. The humpback whale is usually black with white splotches.

The right whale's head is big and lumpy.

Tips for Whale Watching

It is safest to go whale watching from the shore. The next best is to be in a boat that is a safe distance from the whale. Getting too close to the whale could frighten and disturb it. Keeping at a distance keeps the whale safe.

Glossary

ancestor	distant relative from long ago
baleen plates	tough, elastic, fringed sheets that hang down on both sides of a baleen whale's mouth used to strain krill
buoyant	able to float easily
Cretaceous period	the period of geological time when plants evolved and dinosaurs and other reptiles flourished, approximately 65 million years ago
echolocation	a means of locating objects by the use of sound and echo
mammals	warm-blooded animals that breathe air and feed their young milk

Index

air 10, 11
ancestors 16
Antarctic 7
Arctic 7
baleen plates 5
baleen whale/
  baleen whales 4, 5, 10
beaches 19
blowhole/blowholes 10, 11
blubber 7
blue whale 9
calves 7
Cretaceous period 16
dolphins 4, 8, 12, 19
Earth 9
echo 15
echolocation 4, 15
eyesight 15
fish 4
flippers 20
food 4, 15
groups 12
habitat 20
head/heads 10, 21
hearing 15
humpback whale/
  humpback whales 5, 9, 14, 20
krill 5
leader 13
legs 16

limbs 17
lungs 10, 11
mammal order 8
mammal/mammals 6, 8, 9, 10
milk 6
ocean 9
pilot whales 4
pod 12, 13
porpoises 4, 8, 12
relatives 8
right whale/right whales 5, 9, 20
scientists 14, 16, 19
shrimp 5
skeleton 17
sound/sounds 14, 15
sperm whales 4
squid 4
steam 11
summer 7
toothed whale/
  toothed whales 4, 10, 15
water/waters 7, 8, 9, 11
weight 9
whale/whales 4, 5, 6, 7, 8, 9, 10,
  11, 12, 13, 14, 15, 16, 17, 18, 19, 20,
  21, 22
whale song 14
whale watching 22
young 6